BETWEEN ____

LINES

2 COR 1:13

TEDDY E. ASSITER

Senior Link Publishing

Lubbock, Texas

Senior Link Publishing
Lubbock, Texas
www.lubbockseniorlink.com

Between The Lines/ Teddy E. Assiter. —1st ed.
ISBN 979-8-3923962-8-3

Dedicated To:

All who have made the most important decision in their life!

And to my wife, Corky, who read each chapter in this book as it was completed; often giving me a new insight, to what I should write.

Authors Introduction:

Everyone can use a little inspiration, a little reminder of what is truly good, moral and just.

This book, Between The Lines, tells short and easy-to-read stories from the Bible —linked to pithy quotations and scripture.

You will ask yourself, "Is that in the Bible?"

Some of the stories will challenge you to think, and in some cases may touch a soft spot in your heart. It is my hope it will cause you to open your Bibles, and to pray to our Creator every day! Either way this book promises you an expanded vision and new insights.

Just as the Gospel writers wrote about the same person, Jesus —each from a different point of view, these words are linked to the eternal truth of God's Word.

It is not the action of sitting in a pew in church each week that is going to make the world a better place to live —it is the heart of the person sitting in the pew.

We must all love one another, pray for each other —and answer the first question asked to God in Genesis: "Yes, we are our brother's keeper," and our neighbor is all mankind.

Teddy E. Assiter

A note from the author:

The goal of any Bible translation is to convey the meaning and content of the ancient Hebrew, Aramaic, and Greek texts as accurately as possible to contemporary readers; therefore most of the references I use in writing this book are from The New Living Bible.

From the beginning when God and Abraham made a covenant between the two that Abraham would be the father of the Jewish nation (Israel), the focus of many people became to wipe them from the face of the earth. Even in recent times Hitler tried to remove them through gas chambers with no success! Is it because they are "God's chosen people"? The Old Testament tells story after story about the things they have had to do to survive! Their promised land has been taken from them time after time. The most holy city to them is Jerusalem where Solomon built the Temple, where they could worship Him. Part of Jerusalem has been returned to them in 1945, yet the struggle between them and Palestine continues.

One can't say that the Nation of Israel hasn't had warning after warning of their future when they stop worshiping God. Just read Isaiah, Jeremiah, Ezekiel, or any of the other prophets!

Contents

The Prodigal Son 1

Gideon 9

Adam and Eve.. 15

Moses.. 21

John the Baptist.. 29

Joshua... 37

Job 45

Esther.. 53

Solomon.. 59

Ruth.. 65

Daniel 69

Paul... 77

The Twelve 81

Noah 89

Stephen 93

Samson 97

Elijah 101

Mary Magdalene..105

Timothy..109

Satan...113

Psalms...119

Last Chapter 123

[1]

THE PRODIGAL SON

In the fifteenth chapter of the Gospel according to Saint Luke, the parable is told of the lost son; or the prodigal sons, both were prodigal!

It is clear a man has two sons. We will never know the difference in their ages, and he may have had daughters too. I suspect there was very little difference in the age of his sons; maybe, a year or two. During their youth and teen years the brothers could have been very close to each other —then as manhood was reached it is possible the older brother aided in the awareness to his brother that they were sons and heirs of a very wealthy father. He could have influenced his brother to ask for the portion of goods that would fall to him knowing his father would divide with both of them.

After their father gave them their inheritance; it is possible the older brother caused his brother to leave. I can hear him bossing his brother and telling him, "If you don't like me telling you what to do — then why don't you leave?" The Bible says: "And not many days after the younger son packed all his belongings and moved to a distant land."

In this far country we are told this prodigal son wasted his inheritance with riotous living. Again, we can only guess at the number of years it took him to go broke. I am sure the father had tried to talk his son out of leaving home, but wealth in hand the son stepped into rebellion.

The rift between the brothers could have developed during this time. As he left home he was probably mad; maybe, even told them he never wanted to see any of them again in his anger.

As Christians, anytime we get outside the will of God or do our own thing without Divine Guidance — we are in a foreign country! I suggest he was in rebellion for a long time. The Lord has a way of working circumstances for each of us —tailor-made to deal with things in our lives that the Lord wants brought to the surface and for us to deal with. After his money was gone, his friends were gone; and there he was alone and broke.

Being a homeless person in a far country was bad. In order to eat he went and joined himself to a citizen of this country, who gave him work, sending him into the field to feed swine. In the field feeding the swine he begins to reckon with himself, on what has happened to him. He discovers everything has gone downhill since he left his father's authority:

He had no one who loved him!

He had no one who had his best interest at heart!

He had no one to give him guidance!

In reckoning with himself he realized he needed to be under authority. We do not know how long he fed swine for this citizen; but, during this time he becomes aware of his circumstance — of what had happened to his life. Why it had happened: and that no one was to blame except himself. He is learning the facts of life the hard way — his own experience. He learns only he oversees his destiny. He asks himself; how many hired servants of my father have bread enough to spare and I perish with hunger? Realization comes to him that he is still his father's son. I will go home to my father. I suspect when he left home he wrote his father off as a dumb ol' dad. He was unaware if his brother was still alive; if he had married and had children — and he really didn't care! Little did he realize his father had inquired about him from every foreigner he met, and was praying that he was safe, and would return someday!

Returning home was not going to be easy, he didn't know if his father was still alive; maybe, all he would find would be his older brother who surely did not want him to return. He promised himself that he would ask his father for forgiveness and tell him what a fool he had been. In this repentance in his mind and heart, he realizes how very much he loves his father, and even how he misses his brother too. His father saw him when he was a great way off and had compassion and ran and he embraced and kissed him. It would have been so easy to forget asking forgiveness, but he kept the promise he made to himself and asks his father to forgive him. He told his dad what a fool he had been, and that he was not worthy to be called his son.

Do you suspect there might have been a moment of doubt as he saw his father running to greet him? Seeing his ol' man rushing toward him, it would have been easy for him to just let his father welcome him home; and to enjoy the benefits of the household. We must admire this young prodigal: He did exactly as he said he was going to do. Before he could finish asking forgiveness his father yelled to a servant: "Bring forth the best robe, and put on his hand a ring, and shoes on his feet, and bring hither the fatted calf, and kill it. And let us eat and be merry: For this my son was dead and is alive again; he was lost and is found!"

Let us consider some facts about the father. The father did not have to divide or give the sons their inheritance when it was asked. He could have said no, you are too young to know how to manage your inheritance. We Christians have an inheritance today, and I think Our Heavenly Father wants us to claim it. He gave to them freely to use wisely, or misuse — no strings attached. Our Lord freely gives us our inheritance; and the only way we can keep from misusing it is to stay close to His Guidance. I suspect the father had even told his servants to watch for the son to return. There was really no need for anyone to watch because I suspect the older brother had told the servants not to watch for him, because he had received word he had died. Needless to say, the love of the father is overwhelming!

A way to remember this prodigal son is to divide his youth into six parts: Each begins with the letter "R": Renewal! Rebellion! Reckoning! Realization! Repentance! And Restoration!

With the older brother it's a different story. Coming in from working in the field he hears music and calls to a servant and asks, "What's going on inside?" He is told that his brother who had been gone for years had now come home, and his father killed the fatted calf, because he received him safe and sound, "Come rejoice with us, your brother is safe and at home."

However, from there the older son shows his true colors. His greed, hate, lying, selfishness and other hang-ups all come to light.

The Bible says, "The elder son was in the field." Remember, this was the older son of a very wealthy man. There was no reason for him to be in the field working; unless, he had done some riotous living of his own. Could it be possible he had lost all his money too? Had to move back into his father's house, and work as an overseer? Now he is told his younger brother has returned home and being treated like a king. It must have hit him like a sledgehammer when he was told —now after all these years, his brother shows up! He becomes very angry and refuses to go in!

There is still more to this story. If things had been right between him and his father, there would have been no need to ask a servant what was going on. He would have rejoiced with his father that his brother was home and safe! This happens to us Christians too.

Sometimes we find it hard to rejoice with other Christians when something good happens to them.

How hard it is for a childless couple who wants a baby to attend a christening —or attend the party of a fellow worker who received the promotion you felt you deserved and were going to get? It is far easier to weep with those who weep than rejoice when there is rejoicing!

His father saw him come in from work, and ran to him too, giving him the good news of his brother's return. His father begged him to come celebrate with the family. In his refusal he told his Dad "Why throw a party when this son of yours (not my brother) who has squandered your money on prostitutes comes home." How could this son have known how his brother spent his money? Shows the thinking of how he would have spent his money. We do not know how long the father and son were outside discussing. I like to think that everything surfaced from this meeting. I can see the heartwarming picture as the father put his arms around this son and they go inside together. How the brothers rejoice at seeing each other!

There is joy in this household as all are reconciled.

[2]

GIDEON

In the sixth and seventh chapters of Judges is the story of how Gideon becomes Israel's Judge. The Israelites did evil in the Lord's sight. So, the Lord handed them over to the Midianites for seven years. The Midianites were so cruel that the Israelites made hiding places for themselves in the mountains, caves and strongholds. Then the angel of the Lord came and watched Gideon as he was threshing wheat at the bottom of a winepress to hide the grain from the Midianites. Here the angel of the Lord appeared to him and said, "Mighty hero, the Lord is with you." No doubt this angel had a sense of humor. Then Gideon asked what I think is a very shrewd question: "If the Lord is with us, why has all this happened to us? And where are all the miracles our ancestors told us about?" It seems this angel was the Lord Himself and He said to Gideon, "Go with your strength you have, and rescue Israel from the Midianites. I am sending you!" "But Lord" Gideon replied, "how can I rescue Israel? My clan is the weakest in the whole tribe of Manasseh, and I am the least in my entire family?" It was not that Gideon was just in an arguing mood, this was his first time to be called on to do something for the Lord and he wanted assurance that this was not just a dream.

If I were in Gideon's place, I would have doubts and questions too. Gideon came up with a plan, and asked the angel, "If you are truly going to help me, show me a sign to prove that it is really the Lord speaking to me." After seeing a sign, Gideon felt better about the situation, until that night, when the Lord appeared again and told him to pull down his father's altar to Baal and cut down the Asherah pole standing beside it. Gideon thought for a few minutes then spoke to the Lord and told him he could not do that — that altar was his dad's pride and joy, very dear to him! This must be done. He was told. Then build an altar to the Lord using as fuel the wood from the Asherah pole he had cut down.

So, Gideon took ten of his servants and did as the Lord had commanded. But he did it at night because he was afraid of the other members of his father's household and of the people in the town. When it was discovered the next day what had been destroyed and who had done it, the men of the town demanded that Gideon must die.

Meanwhile the armies of Midian, Amalek, and the people of the east formed an alliance against Israel. Now, instead of just defeating the Midianites there was an alliance that the Israelites faced. Gideon became confused; was it really him God had picked to rescue Israel? He needed more confirmation and proof he was the chosen one! Again he asks for a sign: "God, If you are truly going to use me to rescue Israel as you promised prove it to me this way, I will put a fleece on the threshing floor tonight. If the fleece is wet with dew in the morning, but the ground is dry, then I will know that you are going to help me rescue Israel as you promised."

When Gideon got up early the next morning, he squeezed the fleece and wrung out a whole bowlful of water. This should have been proof enough for Gideon! In this way I relate to Gideon in my own life. There are times when I have asked for a sign — but received none.

Then I remember that after the baptism of Jesus, He was given temptations by the devil, and He told Satan, "The Scriptures also say You must not test the Lord your God".

Did Gideon not now have the proof he asked for? Then Gideon said to God, "Please don't be angry with me, but let me make one more request. Let me use the fleece for one more test. This time let the fleece remain dry while the ground around it is wet with dew." So that night God did as Gideon asked. The fleece was dry in the morning, but the ground was covered with dew. Just the confirmation I needed Gideon thought to himself. Gideon called his army together and told them they were going to war and would defeat the alliance that has been formed!

God took one glance of the army Gideon had formed and told him, "You have too many warriors. If I let all of you fight the Midianites, the Israelites will boast to me that they saved themselves by their own strength." "Wait a minute," Gideon replied. "I need very fighter I have, and could use more, remember the formed alliance?" "No" the Lord told Gideon, "If I am going to help you win, it must be done my way! So, tell your soldiers, whoever is timid or afraid, to go home." When Gideon did this, 22,000 of them went home, leaving only 10,000 who were willing to fight.

"You still have too many," God told Gideon.

"Lord", Gideon replied, "They out number us now ten to one." "Still too many" Gideon was told. "Bring the rest of your army down to the spring, and I will test them to determine who will go with you and who will not." At the end of the test there were only 300 men left.

This is just the start of Gideon's life —there is a lot more! But you must go to your Bible and read it for yourself!

[3]

ADAM AND EVE

"And there was war in heaven; Michael and Gabriel, and their angels fought against the dragon; and the dragon fought and his angels and prevailed not; neither was their place found anymore in heaven. And the great dragon was cast out, that old serpent, called the Devil, and Satan, which deceive the whole world; he was cast out unto the earth, and his angels were cast out with him." Revelation 12:7-9

"How art thou fallen from heaven O Lucifer, Son of the morning! How art thou cut down to the ground." Isaiah 14:12

Meanwhile in the Garden of Eden is Adam admiring all the beauty God has made. His work for this day is to give all the animals a name. Day after day, God sees how lonely Adam is with no one to talk to, so he takes a rib from Adam and creates a woman.

Adam is very pleased, he gives her the name of Eve, she is the most beautiful thing he has seen.

"Look at the delicious fruit on the tree, let us eat" she tells Adam. "No, not of that tree" Adam explains, "for God has said that the day we eat of it that we will die." "Nonsense!" comes a voice from behind them, "God knows the very day you eat of that tree that your eyes will be open, that you will become like God." From the very beginning it was Satan's purpose to overthrow the laws of God. To accomplish this he entered his rebellion against the Creator and though he was cast out of heaven, he has continued the same warfare on earth.

Satan takes the fruit from the tree of knowledge when he and Eve are alone. "This is very yummy, best I'm ever tasted. Here, have a bite." Eve is very pleased with the taste and runs to give Adam a bite. "That is good, from which tree did it come?" On being told which tree it had come from Adam responded, "Woman, what have you done?" "The fruit was given to me and he ate and told me how very sweet it was," Eve explained.

"Adam! Adam! Adam! Eve!" came the voice of God, "Where are you?" "Over here" Adam answered. "We heard you in the garden and were afraid, so we hid ourselves because we were naked." "Who told you, you were naked" asked God. "Have you eaten fruit from the tree that I commanded you not to eat?" Adam explained, "It was Eve who gave it to me." "It's not my fault" Eve explained, "It was he over there that gave it to me to eat."

God turned to Satan; "Because thou hast done this, thou art cursed above all cattle, and above every beast of the field; upon your belly you shall crawl, and dust you will eat all the days to come. And I will put enmity between you and the woman, and between thy seed and her seed. I will greatly multiply her sorrow and her conception; in sorrow she shall bring forth children; and her desire shall be to her husband, and he shall rule over her. And to you Adam, because you ate of the fruit she gave you, I curse the ground you walk on. No more can you live in the Garden of Eden. You must now work the ground for food to eat. There will be thorns and thistles, you will eat the herbs of the field you grow by the sweat on your face, later you will have bread to eat from the wheat you have sown."

Take a moment to turn to and read chapter 12 in the Book of Revelation.

"Now, Adam had sexual relations with his wife, Eve, and she became pregnant. When she gave birth to Cain, she said, 'With the Lord's help I have produced a man!' Later she gave birth to his brother and named him Abel."

As the boys grew up, each had an interest different from his brother. Abel loved animals and became a shepherd. Cain helped his father cultivate the soil and became a farmer.

They had each been taught from childhood to each year give a portion of their labor to the Lord!

When it was time for the harvest, Cain presented some of his crops to the Lord. Abel also brought a gift — the best of the firstborn lambs from his flock. The Lord accepted Abel and his gift, but he did not accept Cain and his gift.

It appears to me that both did what was expected of them. Why would the Lord accept one, and refuse the other? The Lord knew that while working in the field that Satan had approached Cain several times: telling him how unfair he was being treated by his family. This made Cain very angry.

"Why are so angry?" the Lord asked Cain, "you will be accepted if you do what is right. But if you refuse to do what is right, then watch out! Sin is crouching at the door, eager to control you." One day Cain suggested to his brother, "Let's go out into the field." And while they were in the field, Cain attacked his brother, and killed him.

Afterward the Lord asked Cain, "Where is your brother?" "I don't know," Cain responded.

"Am I my brother's keeper?" All throughout the Bible, especially the New Testament, this question is asked.

The Lord cursed and banished him from the ground, which had swallowed his brother's blood. "No longer will the ground yield good crops for you, no matter how hard you work! From now own you will be a homeless wanderer on earth". Then Cain left the Lord's presence and settled in the land of Nod. Previously God had created Nod, and placed humans there. It was there that Cain took a wife, and had children. Genesis continues with the descendants of Cain.

"Adam had sexual relations with his wife again she gave birth to another son. She named him Seth. When Seth grew up, he had a son and named him Enosh: At that time people first began to worship the Lord by name."

This is the written account of the descendants of Adam. When God created human beings, He made them to be like himself. He created them male and female, and he blessed them and called them human.

[4]

MOSES

A new king came to power in Egypt, who knew nothing about Joseph or what he had done. The king called to the attention of the people that the Israelites had grown in numbers that outnumbered them and were stronger than the Egyptians. He said that they must plan to keep them from growing even more. So, the Egyptians made the Israelites their slaves. They appointed brutal slave drivers over them hoping to wear them down with crushing labor. But the more the Egyptians oppressed them, the more the Israelites multiplied in numbers. The king knew he had to do something to control the population and he gave the order that when an Israelite gave birth to a boy baby, he was to be thrown into the Nile River.

During this time, a man and woman from the tribe of Levi got married. The woman became pregnant and gave birth to a son and was able to keep him hidden for three months. But when she could no longer hide him, she got a basket, put him in it, and laid it among the reeds along the bank of the Nile River.

Soon Pharaoh's daughter came to the river to take a bath. When the princess saw the basket among the reeds, she sent her maid to get it for her. The little boy was crying and she felt sorry for him. "This must be one of the Hebrew children," she said. Then the baby's sister approached the princess. This girl asked, "Should I go and find one of the Hebrew women to nurse the baby for you?" "Yes do!" the princess replied. So, the girl went and called the baby's mother. "Take this baby and nurse him for me," the princess told the baby's mother. "I will pay you for your help." So, the woman took the baby home and nursed him.

Later, when the boy was older, his mother brought him back to Pharaoh's daughter, who adopted him as her own son. The princess named him Moses, for she explained, "I lifted him out of the water."

Many years later Prince Moses observed a Hebrew slave being beat with a whip, he killed the Egyptian and hid the body in the sand. Pharaoh and Moses had never had a close relationship, even though he was his grandson. Pharoah only let Moses live in the palace because of his love for his daughter. Pharaoh despised Moses because of his ability not to speak plainly! When Pharaoh was told what had happen, he tried to kill Moses! Moses fled Egypt and went to live in the land of Midian.

When Moses arrived in Midian, he sat down beside a well. Now the priest of Midian had seven daughters who came as usual to draw water and fill the water troughs for their father's flocks. But some other shepherds came and chased them away. So, Moses jumped up and rescued the girls from the shepherds. Then he drew water for their flocks.

When the girls returned to Reuel, their father ask why they had returned so soon. He was told what had happen at the well, and how this Egyptian had rescued them from the shepherds. "Where is he now? He asks his daughters "Why did you leave him there? Go find him and ask him to come eat with us." The daughters were delighted to invite such a good-looking man to their home. Moses accepted their invitation and settled down to live with them.

In time Reuel (who sometimes went by the name, Jethro) gave Moses his daughter Zipporah, to be his wife. Later she gave birth to a son and Moses named him Gershom. More years passed and then Pharaoh died. But the Israelites continue to groan under their burden of slavery. They cried out for help, and their cry rose to God.

God heard their groaning, and he remembered his covenant promise to Abraham, Isaac, and Jacob. God looked down on the people of Israel and knew it was time to act.

One day Moses was tending the flock of his father-in-law. There the angel of the Lord appeared to him in a blazing fire from the middle of a bush. Moses stared in amazement. Though the bush was engulfed in flames, it did not burn. As Moses approached the bush for a closer look, God called to him from the middle of the bush, "Moses! Moses!" "Here I am!" Moses replied. "Do not come any closer". The Lord warned "Take off your sandals, for you are standing on holy ground."

The Lord told Moses He was aware of the suffering of His people at the hand of the Egyptians. And now, with the help of Moses, they were going to be freed and have their own land.

If you the reader of this wants to know how this is going to happen, read Exodus chapters three through fourteen, in your Bible.

The Israelites saw the mighty power of God that was unleashed against the Egyptians, they were filled with awe before him. They put their faith in the Lord and in his servant Moses.

On their journey to their promised land, slowly Satan put doubts into the minds of all 600,000 men plus all the women and children that had been delivered out of Egypt. The people began to complain about everything: from the water they had to drink to the manna that they received daily. "If only the Lord had killed us back in Egypt," they moaned. There we sat around pots filled with meat and ate all the bread they wanted. Also, they complained about Moses and Aaron.

At this time Moses' father-in-law, Jethro had heard about everything God had done for Moses, and his people, the Israelites. He sent a message to Moses telling him that he was coming to visit him in the wilderness. On his arrival, Jethro observed everything his son-in-law had to do for the people. "This is not good!" Jethro exclaimed. "You're going to wear yourself out —and the people, too. This job is too heavy a burden for you to handle all by yourself. Moses listened to the advice of his father-in-law and followed his suggestions. He chose capable men from all over Israel and appointed them as leaders over the people.

Two months after the Israelites left Egypt they arrived in the wilderness of Sinai. There Moses climbed the mountain to appear before God. The Lord called to him from the mountains and said,

"Give these instructions to the family of Jacob; announce it to the descendants of Israel. Moses was told to prepare the Israelites for a visit from Him, and from Mt. Sinai God gave the people instructions. God called Moses to the mountain again and they made a Covenant.

When the people saw how long it was taking Moses to come back down the mountain, they gathered around Aaron. "Come on," they said, "make us some gods who can lead us. We don't know what happened to this fellow, Moses." The people brought gold to Aaron, and he made them a golden calf to worship.

The Lord told Moses, "Quick! Go down the mountain! Your people have corrupted themselves. How quickly they have turned away from the way I commanded them to live. They have melted down gold and made a calf, and they have bowed down and sacrificed to it. Now leave me alone so My fierce anger can blaze against them, and I will destroy all of them."

Moses reasoned with the Lord, why should He destroy His people whom he had delivered out of Egypt? So, the Lord changed His mind about the terrible disaster He had threatened to bring on his people. Moses was given the procedures to do all things.

The things that happen to Moses in the years to come are recorded in the books of the Bible: Exodus, Leviticus, Numbers and Deuteronomy.

Moses was not permitted to enter the "promised land". It is my belief that Moses died on Mt. Sinai and his body is buried there.

[5]

JOHN THE BAPTIST

It began just as the prophet Isaiah had written: "Look, I am sending my messenger ahead of you, and he will prepare your way. He is a voice shouting in the wilderness. Prepare the way for the Lord's coming! Clear the road for him!"

When Herod was king of Judea, there was a Jewish priest named Zechariah. He was a member of the priestly order of Abijah, and his wife, Elizabeth was also from the priestly line of Aaron. They were both righteous in God's eyes, careful to obey all the Lord's commandments and regulations. They had no children because Elizabeth was unable to conceive, and they both were very old. For years Elizabeth had tried to no avail to become pregnant, and now time had ran out for them, as the age had passed them by when Elizabeth could have conceived. One week when it was Zechariah's order to have the duty at the temple, he was in the sanctuary, when an angel of the Lord appeared to him. "Don't be afraid Zechariah! God has heard your prayer. Your wife, Elizabeth, will give you a son, and you are to name him John. You will have great joy and gladness, and many will rejoice at his birth, for he will be great in the eyes of the Lord. He must never touch wine or other alcoholic drinks. He will be filled with the Holy Spirit, even before his birth. He will have the spirit and power of Elijah. He will prepare the people for the coming of the Lord." Zechariah said to the angel, "How can I be sure this will happen, I'm an old man now, and my wife is also along in years."

Then the angel said, "I am Gabriel! I stand in the very presence of God. It was He who sent me to bring you the good news! But now, since you don't believe what I say, you will be unable to speak until your son is born."

Meanwhile, the people were waiting for Zechariah to come out of the sanctuary, wondering why it was taking him so long. He came out and was unable to speak. From his silence and gestures, they assumed he had had a vision. Soon afterwards his wife became pregnant and went into seclusion for five months.

Before John was born, God sent Gabriel to visit a virgin named Mary. He told her she had found favor with God and would have a son who was to be given the name, Jesus. Gabriel told Mary that a relative of hers had become pregnant in her old age, so Mary went to visit Elizabeth. Elizabeth told her that when she heard her greetings that the baby in her womb jumped for joy!

This is being used today in the fight over abortion: When does life began? Many claim that life begins at birth, while others claim it is at conception and abortion is murder. The fight continues and I doubt if it will ever be settled, regardless of the laws we make. In some parts of the world, when a child is born their age is one. Others, give their age as one, three months after birth. And we in this country celebrate the child as one year old on the anniversary of their birth. My thought on this subject is that life has begun when the woman's normal menstrual cycle has stopped.

When it was time for Elizabeth's baby to be born, she gave birth to a son. When the child was eight days old, many came for the circumcision ceremony, thinking the child should be named after his father Zechariah. When Elizabeth told his name would be John, they used gestures to ask the child's father what his name was to be. Zechariah motioned for a writing tablet, and to everyone's surprise he wrote, "His name is John." Instantly, Zechariah could speak again, and began praising God!

In the fifteenth year of the reign of Tiberius, a message was sent from God to John who was living in the wilderness that it was time to begin paving the way for Jesus. Then John went from place to place on both sides of the Jordan River preaching that people should be baptized to show they had repented of their sins and turned to God to be forgiven.

As the crowds came to John for baptism, he said, "You brood of snakes! Who warned you to flee God's coming wrath? Prove by the way you live that you have repented of your sins and turned to God." The crowds asked, "What should we do to show we have repented?" John replied, "If you have two shirts, give one to the poor. If you have food, share it with those who are hungry."

John used many such warnings as he announced the Good News to the people. John also publicly criticized Herod Antipas, the ruler of Galilee for marrying Herodias, his brother's wife, and for many other wrongs he had done. Later he was put in prison because he constantly referred to the sins of the ruler.

One day, when the crowds were being baptized, John looked up and saw Jesus coming toward him and said to the crowd, "Behold, the lamb of God is coming, who will take away the sins of the world. I am not worthy enough even to untie the sandals on His feet." I baptize you with water, but he will baptize you with the Holy Spirit! Why are you coming to me Cousin?" "To be baptized," was Jesus' reply. "It is I who should be baptized by you." As John raised Jesus out of the water, the heavens opened and the Holy Spirit in bodily form descended on him like a dove.

And a voice from heaven said, "You are my dearly loved Son, and you bring me great joy." After Jesus was given temptations by Satan, He began His ministry.

Herod got tired of all that John saying about him and had him put in prison because he refused to shut his mouth about him.

John had often been asked if he was the Messiah. "No," he always replied, "I am only preparing the way for him."

In prison, John's disciples told him everything that Jesus was doing. Maybe it was because John was off his regular diet of locusts and wild honey that he enjoyed in the wilderness that he called for two of his disciples and sent them to Jesus to ask him, "Are you the Messiah we've been expecting, or should we keep looking for someone else?

I ask myself, what was he thinking? John knew the answer to this question. As-a-matter of fact he knew it even when they played together as kids! Jesus told John's disciples to report to him everything they had seen him do.

After John's disciples left, Jesus began talking about him to the crowds. "What kind of man did you go into the wilderness to see? Was he a weak reed, swayed by every breath of the wind? Or were you expecting to see a man dressed in expensive clothes? No, people who wear beautiful clothes live in luxury and are found in palaces. Were you looking for a prophet? Yes, and John is more than a prophet. I tell you, of all who have ever lived, none is great then John. Yet even the least person in the Kingdom of God is greater than he."

Herod wanted to kill John, but he was afraid of a riot because all the people believed John to be a prophet. But at a birthday party for Herod, Herodias's daughter preformed a dance that greatly pleased him, so he promised with a vow to give her anything she wanted. She could not think of anything she wanted, so she asked her mother, "What should I ask for?" At her mother's urging, the girl said, "I want the head of John the Baptist on a tray. The king regretted what he had said, but because of the vow he had made in front of his guest, he issued the necessary order.

At this point Herod could have said "No!" "I will give you something else, how about half of my kingdom?" John was beheaded in the prison and his head was brought on a tray and given to the girl, who took it to her mother.

[6]

JOSHUA

The time came when Moses was 120 years old. God had told him he could not enter the promised land, so he knew it was time for a change of command! Moses prayed that he would choose someone the Lord would approve of to lead the people into their own land. Several men seemed to be strong enough, but there was only one he felt was able to lead the Israelites.

Then Moses called for Joshua, and as all Israel watched he said to him, "Be strong and courageous! For you will lead these people into the land that the Lord swore to their ancestors he would give them. You are the one who will divide it among them as their grants of land. Do not be afraid or discouraged, for the Lord will personally go ahead of you, He will be with you; He will never fail you nor abandon you.

Be careful to obey all the instruction Moses gave you. Do not deviate from them, turning either to the right or to the left. Then you will be successful in everything you do."

If you are interested in knowing all the instruction Moses gave to Joshua, search the Scriptures and see for yourself. Start reading in the 31st chapter of Deuteronomy.

Then Joshua commanded the officers of Israel, "Go through the camp and tell the people to get their provisions ready. In three days, you will cross the Jordan River and take possession of the land the Lord your God is giving you. Then Joshua called together the tribes of Reuben, Gad, and the half-tribe of Manasseh. He told them, "Remember what Moses, the servant of the Lord, commanded you": The Lord your God is giving you a place to rest. He has given you this land. Your wives, children and livestock may remain here in the east side of the Jordan River, but your strong warriors, fully armed, must lead the other tribes across the Jordan to help them conquer their territory. Stay with them until the Lord gives them rest, as he has given you rest, and until they, too, possess the land the Lord your God has given them. Only then may you return and settle here on the east side of the Jordan River in the land that Moses, the servant of the Lord assigned to you;"

They answered Joshua, "We will do whatever you command us, and we will go wherever you send us. We will obey you just as we obeyed Moses. Anyone who rebels against your orders and does not obey your words and everything you command will be put to death. So be strong and courageous!"

Then Joshua secretly sent out two spies from the Israel camp at Acacia Grove. He instructed them, "Scout out the land on the other side of the Jordan River, especially around Jericho." So, the two men set out and came to the house of a prostitute named Rahab and stayed there that night. Is this part of the training to be a spy, to spend time with a prostitute? Hope the price of the stay was reasonable. The king of Jericho got word that some spies had come to spy out the city and were staying at the home of a prostitute name Rahab. Police were sent to her home but found no men there. Rahab had hidden the two men, but she replied, "Yes, two men were here, they left the town at dusk, as the gates were about to close." Rahab had hidden the men on the roof. That night Rahab went to where the men were hiding and told them it was safe to come down. She told them all the people in Jericho were afraid of the Israelites because they had heard how the Lord made a dry path for them through the Red Sea when they left Egypt and all the plagues on the Egyptians. Everyone in the city is living in terror. No one in the city has the courage to fight after hearing such things. For the Lord your God is the supreme God of the heavens above and the earth below. Rahab told the two men, "Now swear to me by your God, that you will be kind to me and my family, since I have helped you. Give me some guarantee that when Jericho is conquered, you will let members of my family live." "We offer our own lives as a guarantee for your safety," the men agreed.

Rahab's house was built into the town wall and she let the men down by a rope through a window for their escape. Before the men left, they told her that her family would be safe only if they followed these instructions: when we come into the land, you must leave this scarlet rope hanging from the window through which you let us escape. All your family must stay inside this house. If any of them go out into the streets, they will be killed.

The spies returned and reported to Joshua what had happened to them. "The Lord has given us the whole land," they said, "for all the people in the land are terrified of us."

Joshua made a search of the camp to be sure that the generation of Israelites that had worshiped and bowed down to the gold calf Aaron had made had died. When he was satisfied not one of them remained alive, he had the horn blown to bring them all together.

Early the next morning Joshua and all the Israelites left Acacia Grove and the banks of the Jordan River, where they camped before crossing. Three days later the Israelite officers went through the camp giving these instructions to the people, when you see the Levitical priests carrying the Ark of the Covenant of the Lord your God, move out from your positions and follow them. "Since you have never traveled this way before, they will guide you. Stay about a half mile behind them, keeping a clear distance between you and the Ark. Make sure you don't come any closer."

Then Joshua told the people. "Purify yourselves for tomorrow the Lord will do great wonders among you." The next morning Joshua said to the priests, "Lift up the Ark of the Covenant and lead the people across river." And so, they started out and went ahead of the people.

The Lord told Joshua, "Today I will begin to make you a great leader in the eyes of the Israelites. They will realize that I am with you, just as I was with Moses. "Give this command to the priests who carry the Ark of the Covenant: When you reach the banks of the Jordan River, take a few steps into the river and stop there."

Joshua told the Israelites, "Come and listen to what the Lord your God says. Today you will know that the living God is among you. He will drive out the Canaanites, Hittites, Hivites, Perizzites, Girgashites, Amorites, and Jebusites ahead of you. Look, the Ark of the Covenant, which belongs to the Lord of the whole earth, will lead you across the Jordan River! Now choose twelve men from the tribes of Israel, one from each tribe. The priests will carry the Ark of the Lord, the Lord of all the earth. As soon as their feet touch the water, the flow of water will be cut off upstream and the river will stand up like a wall." It happened just as Joshua said it would, and the whole nation of Israel crossed the Jordan on dry ground.

It is hard for me to understand why God always keeps the feet of His people dry. I wonder if they might serve Him better if He let them swim once in a while! When all the Amorite kings west to the Jordan and all the Canaanite kings who live along the Mediterranean coast heard how the Lord had dried up the Jordan River so the people of Israel could cross, they lost heart and were paralyzed with fear because of them.

When Joshua was near the town of Jericho he looked up and saw a man standing in front of him with a sword in hand, Joshua went up to him and

demanded, "Are you friend or foe?" "Neither one," he
replied, "I am the commander of the Lord's army."
At this, Joshua fell with his face to the ground in
reverence. "I am at your command," Joshua said.
"What do you want your servant to do?" The commander of the Lord's army replied, "Take off your
sandals, for the place you are standing is holy." Joshua did as he was told.

The commander told Joshua that the time had
come for his people to capture the city of Jericho.
"How can we do this?" Joshua asked. "The spies I
sent failed to tell me that the walls of the city of Jericho were over twenty feet high and the gates are sel-
dom open to strangers."

The commander of God's army told Joshua he
would tell them how it was to be done. "You, and the
few men you have that are willing to fight should
march around the town once a day for six days, seven
priests will walk ahead of the Ark that is being carried, each with a ram's horn in their hand. On the
seventh day you are to march around the town seven
times with the priests blowing their horns. At a large
blast from the horns all your people will shout! And
the walls of Jericho will collapse."

It happened just the way Joshua had been told. As
the walls fell there was no need to rush in and kill the
people because each was holding a white flag. The

flag made no difference for the Lord had told the Israelites to kill them all. Then Joshua noticed that a small part of the wall was still standing with a scarlet rope hanging from the window. Joshua told the two spies, "Keep your promise. Go to the prostitutes and bring out all her family." Rahab and her family were taken to a safe place then the Israelites burned the town and everything in it. Only the things made from silver, gold, bronze, or iron were kept for the treasury of the Lord's house.

There is a lot more that happens to Joshua, but you must read it for yourselves in the book of Joshua in the Bible. There you will read where Joshua asks God to show the Israelite army favor. So, the sun stood still, and the moon stayed in place until the nation of Israel had defeated its enemies.

Near the end of Joshua's life, he told the people to choose for themselves who they would serve in the future, but "As for me and my house, we will serve the Lord."

After this, Joshua, son of Nun, the servant of the Lord, died at the age of 110. They buried him in the land he had been allocated, at Timnath- serah in the hill country of Ephraim, north of Mount Gaash.

[7]

JOB

In the land Liz, there lived a very wealthy man. He had seven sons and three daughters and owned 7,000 sheep, 3000 camels, 500 teams of oxen, and 500 female donkeys. In his household there were many servants and he was the wealthiest man in the whole country.

It became a tradition in his family that once a month a son would prepare a feast in their home and the entire family attended.

The man's name was Job. He was very family oriented, often rising in the early morning hours to offer a burnt offering for each of his children. This was an act of purifying for each of them. For Job said to himself, "Perhaps my children have sinned and have cursed God in their hearts." This became his regular practice.

It was a practice in heaven, for members of the heavenly court to present themselves before God. One day Lucifer, the fallen angel came in with them. God asks Satan, "Why are you here?" Satan replied, "I have been patrolling my kingdom on earth, watching everything that is going on, and on all the earth there is only one man I have been unable to control."

"You must be referring to my servant Job," replied the Lord. "He is the finest man in all the earth. He is blameless --a man of complete integrity. He fears me and stays away from all that is evil." Satan replied to the Lord; "Yes, but Job has a good reason to fear You. You have always put a wall of protection around him and his family and all his property. You have made him prosper in everything he does. Look how very rich he is! If you remove the wall of protection around him, he will become one of my followers and curse you to your face!" "All right, you may test him," the Lord said to Satan. "Do whatever you want with everything he possessed, but do not harm him physically."

One day a messenger came to Job with bad news "Your oxen were plowing with the donkey feeding beside them, when the Sabeans raided us. They stole all the animals and killed the farmhands." While he was telling what had happen another messenger arrived with more bad news, "Fire from God has fallen from heaven and burned up your sheep and all the shepherds." Before this messenger finished another messenger arrived with more bad news, "Three bands of Chaldean raiders have stolen all your camels and killed the servants." Just as this messenger finished another messenger arrived with the saddest new of all. "Your sons and daughters were eating at the oldest brother's home. Suddenly, a powerful wind hit the house on all sides. The house collapsed, and all your children are dead!"

Job stood up and tore his robe in grief. Then he shaved his head and fell to the ground to worship. He said "I came naked from my mother's womb, and I will be naked when I leave. The Lord gave me what I had, and the Lord has taken it away. Praise the name of the Lord!" In all of this, Job did not sin by blaming God.

Again, Satan was in attendance when the members of the heavenly court present themselves to the Lord. God said to Satan, "Even though you urged me to let you harm him without cause; Job has maintained his integrity!" Satan replied, "Skin for skin! A man will give up everything he has to save his life. But reach out and take away his health, and he will surely curse you to your face!" "All right, do with him as you please," God told Satan. "But spare his life."

Quickly, Satan struck Job with terrible boils from head to foot. Job's wife said to him, "Are you still trying to maintain your integrity? Curse God and die."

But Job replied, "You talk like a foolish woman. Should we accept only good things from the hand of God and never anything bad?" In all this Job said nothing wrong.

When three of Job's close friends heard of the tragedy that Job had suffered, they got together and traveled to visit him, to comfort and console him. Their names were Eliphaz the Temanite, Bildad the Shuhite, and Zophar the Naamathite. When they arrived, they could hardly recognize him. They sat on the ground with Job for seven day and nights and no one said a word to Job for they saw that his suffering was too great for words.

In their presence Job asked, "Why have I been born. It would have been better that I had died early in life, at least now I would be sleeping with all others that have died. Had I died early in life I would now be at rest. All these things happening to me I can only stand because I love the Lord and He loves me!"

Eliphaz replied to Job. "Will you be patient and let me say a word. In the past you have encouraged many people; you have strengthenedmthose who were weak, your words have supported those who were falling, and you supported those with shaky knees. But now when trouble strikes, you lose heart, you are terrified when it touches you." Eliphaz's response continues for a long time. At the end he tells Job, "If I were you, I would go to God and present my case to him, God does great things, too marvelous to understand. He performs countless miracles. He gives rain to the earth and water for the fields, prosperity to the poor and protection for those who suffer. He rescues the poor as they are being mistreated by others.

Now consider the joy of those corrected by God. Do not despise the discipline of the Almighty when you sin. For though He wounds, He also bandages. He strikes, but His hands also heal."

Eliphaz gives a long response of the things God will do. He concludes, "I have studied life and found all this to be true. Listen to my counsel and apply it to yourself."

Job responds to all this that has been said, "I have nothing to live for. Show me what I have done wrong. Look at me. Would I lie to your face? Stop assuming my guilt, for I have done no wrong. Do you think I am lying? Do I not know the difference between right and wrong?"

Then Job's friend Bildad the Shuhite said to him, "How long will you go on like this? You sound like a blustering wind Does God twist justice? Does the Almighty twist what is right? Your children must have sinned against Him, so their punishment was well deserved. But if you pray to God and seek the favor of the Almighty, He will surely rise up and restore your happy home." Bildad tells Job things he had seen in the past and at the end he tells Job, "God will not reject a person of integrity, such as you; nor will He lend a hand to the wicked. He will once again fill your mouth with laughter and your lips with shouts of joy. Those who hate you will be clothed with shame, and the homes of the wicked will be destroyed."

Then Job spoke, "Yes, I know what you are saying is true in principle. But how can a person be declared innocent in God's sight? If someone wanted to take God to court, would it be possible to answer Him even once in a thousand times? For God is so wise and so mighty. Who has ever challenged Him successfully? Without warning, He moves the mountains, overturning them in His anger. He shakes the earth from its place, and its foundation trembles. If He commands it, the sun will not rise and the stars will not shine. He alone has spread out the heavens and marches on the waves of the sea. He made all the stars —the Bear and Orion, the Pleiades and the constellation of the southern sky. He does great things too marvelous to understand. He performs countless miracles. Who am I, that I should question God? Only God knows the reason all this has happen to me, for I have done nothing wrong!"

Then, Zophar the Naamathite takes his turn to speak: "If you had no wrongdoing, this should not have happen to you. Can a person prove his innocent just by a lot of talking? If only God would speak; and tell you what he thinks! If only He would tell you the secrets of wisdom, for true wisdom is not a simple matter. Listen! God is doubtless punishing you far less than you deserve!

Job takes offense to what is being said by these three. "You people really know everything, do you? And when each of you die, all this wisdom spoken by you will die with you! I know a few things myself, and you're no better than I am!"

His friends, or so-called friends continue with the accusations. Finally, Job tires of all the dialogue and looks up toward heaven: "O God grant me these two things, and then I will be able to face you. Remove your heavy hand from me, and do not terrify me with your awesome presence. Now summon me, and I will answer! Or let me speak to you and you reply. Tell me, what have I done wrong? Show me my rebellion and my sin. Why do you turn away from me? Why do you treat me as your enemy? Tell me about the accusations against me and show me all the sins I have committed! In all this pain I am in God, please just let me die! For I know that my Redeemer lives, and he will stand upon earth at last And after my body has decayed, yet in my body I will see You. I will see you for myself with my own eyes; I will have no more questions or expect any answers to why this has fallen upon me!"

A voice from heaven fills the room, it says, "Eliphaz I am angry with you and your two friends, for you have not spoken accurately about me, as my servant Job has. So, take seven bulls and seven rams and offer a burnt offering for yourselves. My servant Job will pray for you, and I will accept his prayer on your behalf,"

When Job prayed for these three, the Lord restored his health and fortunes. In fact, the Lord gave Job twice as much as before! He restored to life his seven sons and three daughters.

Job lived 140 years after that, living to see four generations of his children and grandchildren. The he died an old man who had lived a long, full life.

[8]

ESTHER

Beware of what can happen when you drink too much wine as King Xerxes can tell you firsthand. King Xerxes ruled his empire from his royal throne at the fortress of Susa. In the third year of his reign, he gave a banquet for all the nobles and officials. He invited all the military officers of Persia and Media as well as the princes and nobles of the 127 provinces he reigned over. The celebration lasted 180 days.

When it was all over, the king gave a banquet for all the people, from the greatest to the least, who were in the fortress of Susa.

We do not have parties today, like they did back then. For one thing we could not afford the price, and there would be few that could take time off from their jobs!

This banquet lasted seven days and everything was beautifully decorated in the courtyard of the palace garden. Drinks were served in gold goblets of many designs, and there was an abundance of royal wine. Reflecting the king's generosity, no limits were placed on the drinking, for the king had instructed all his palace officials to serve each man as much as he wanted.

At the same time, Queen Vashti gave a banquet for the women in the royal palace of King Xerxes.

On the seventh day of the feast when King Xerxes was in high spirits because of the wine, (as we would say today he was drunk) and he told his attendants to bring Queen Vashti to him with the royal crown on her head. He wanted his guests to see and admire the beauty of his wife, the Queen. This was a mistake he would soon regret, for she refused the king's order. She refused to come, and this made him furious.

It was unheard of at this time in history for any woman to fail to obey her husband (times have changed today!).

The king immediately consulted with his wise advisers, who knew all the Persian laws and customs, for he always asked their advice. "What must be done to Queen Vashti?" the king demanded. "What penalty does the law provide for a wife who refuses to obey her husband?"

Memucan, an adviser to the king, answered the king, "Queen Vashti has wronged not only you, but all your guests. She must be punished! If she is not punished women everywhere will begin to despise their husbands when they learn what the Queen has done; all women will praise her for showing them the way and they will start treating their husbands the same way!"

Another advisor to the king suggested. "If it pleases you King Xerxes, I suggest that you issue a written decree, a law of the Persians and Medes that cannot be revoked. It should order that Queen Vashti in her refusal to obey you is no longer Queen and that she be banned from the kingdom and your presence! That you will choose another woman who is more worthy to be queen!" He continued, "When this decree is published husbands, whatever their rank, will receive proper respect and obedience from their wives."

The king thought this made good sense and followed this advice. He sent letters to all parts of the empire, to each province in its own script and language, proclaiming that every man should be the ruler of his own home and say whatever he pleases.

An attendant to the king suggested that a search be made throughout the empire for beautiful, young virgins to come to the palace. Hegai, being in charge of the king's harem, will see that all of them receive beauty treatments. Then the young woman who most pleases the king will become queen. This advice was appealing to the king and he put the plan into effect.

At that time there was a Jewish man in the fortress of Susa named Mordecai, son of Jair. He was from the tribe of Benjamin and was a descendant of Kish and Shimel. His family had been among those who had been exiled from Jerusalem to Babylon by King Nebuchadnezzar. This man had a very beautiful cousin Hadassah, who was also called Esther. When her father and mother died, Mordecai adopted her into his family, and raised her as his own daughter.

As a result of the king's decree, Esther, along with many other young women, was brought to the king's harem at the fortress of Susa and placed in Hegai's care. Hegai was very impressed with Esther and treated her kindly. He quickly ordered a special menu for her and provided her with beauty treatments. He also assigned her seven maids specially chosen from the king's palace and moved her and her maids into the best place in the harem. Just maybe, at this time he realized that she would be chosen to be queen.

Esther had not told anyone of her nationality and family background, because Mordecai had directed her not to do so. Every day Mordecai would take a walk near the courtyard of the harem to find out about Esther and what was happening to her.

Before each young woman was taken to king's bed, she was given the prescribed twelve months of beauty treatments — six months with oil of myrrh, followed with special perfumes and ointments. When it was one of the women's turn to spend the night with the king, the next morning she would be brought to the second harem where the king's wives lived. There she would be under the care of Shaashgaz, who oversaw the king's concubines. She would never go to the king again unless he specifically requested her by name. As these women entertained the king, they were given the right to request from him anything they wanted. When it was Esther's turn to go to the king, she accepted the advice of Hegai. She asked for nothing.

Esther was taken to King Xerxes at the royal palace in early winter of the seventh year of his reign and the king loved Esther more than any of the other women. He was so delighted with her that he set the royal crown on her head and declared her Queen.

To celebrate the occasion, he gave a great banquet in Esther's honor. Esther continued to keep her family background and nationality a secret. Mordecai became an official of the palace. One day as Mordecai was on duty at the king's gate, he heard two men,

Bigthana and Teresh, who guarded the door to the king's private quarter, plotting to assassinate the king. He gave this information to Queen Esther. She then told the king about it and gave Mordecai credit for the report. When an investigation was made and Mordecai's story was found to be true, these two men were impaled on a sharpened pole.

To learn how it was Esther who saved the Jewish nation, you must read it for yourself. In the book of Esther in your Bible reads chapters four thru 10.

[9]

Solomon

David had angered God when he ordered a census to be taken of all of Israel, and God punished Israel for it. Then David said to God, "I have sinned greatly by taking this census. Please forgive my guilt for doing this foolish thing." Then the Lord spoke to Gad, David's advisor.

This was the message. "Go and say to David, this is what the Lord says: I will give you three choices. Choose one of these punishments and I will inflict it on you." The choices were:

1. Three years of famine.

2. Three months of destruction by the sword of your enemies.

3. Three days of severe plague as the angel of the Lord brings devastation throughout the land of Israel.

David chooses the third one; so the Lord sent a plague upon Israel, and 70,000 people died as a result. Witnessing what was happening, David put on burlap to show his deep distress and fell face down on the ground. He called to God, "I am the one who called for the census. It is I who has sinned and done wrong! These people are as innocent as sheep —what have they done? O Lord my God, let your anger fall against me and my family, but do not destroy the people."

The Lord answered the prayer of David and let the dying stop. David asked of the Lord, "What can I do to honor your name?"

"Build me a temple in my name where my people may come and pray and worship me," replied the Lord. "This I will do," David told the Lord. "It will be a magnificent structure that will become famous throughout the world!"

"You are not the one to build this temple," the Lord told David, "You have the blood of the 70,000 who died because of your sin. The temple will be built by your son, Solomon."

David said to the Lord, "My son, Solomon is still young and inexperienced and knows nothing about construction! It will take years to get all the supplies and materials together to build the temple. If it pleases you, Lord. May I have an architect began drawing the plans, and start the collection of materials needed?"

"Solomon, my son," David said. "Learn to know the God of your ancestors, worship and serve him with all your heart and a willing mind."

David, son of Jesse, reigned over all Israel for forty years. Then King David passed the responsibility to his son Solomon.

The Lord appeared to Solomon, the new leader of Israel and said, "What do you want of me? Ask, and I will give it to you!" Solomon replied, "Give me the wisdom and knowledge to lead the people properly, for who could possibly govern this great people of yours?"

God said to Solomon, "Because your greatest desire is to help your people, and you did not ask for wealth, riches, fame, or even the death of your enemies or a long life, but rather you asked for wisdom and knowledge to properly govern my people —I will certainly give you the wisdom and knowledge you requested. And I will also give you wealth, riches, and fame such as no other king has had before you or will ever have in the future!"

Solomon begins to build the temple to honor God. Solomon asks for help from King Hiram at Tyre. Not only did King Hiram send materials to Solomon, but he sends him a master craftsman named Huram-abi.

This man was the first Grand Master of the Masonic Lodge of free masons today!

Solomon began to build the Temple of the Lord in Jerusalem on Mount Moriah. As the temple was completed and furnished, Solomon ordered the Ark of the Lord's Covenant that was located in the City of David, also known as Zion, to be brought to the temple in Jerusalem. At the dedication of the temple, Solomon said a prayer appealing to God. God said, "some of my people are sinning again, if they continue to do this, I might shut up the heavens so that no rain will fall, or command grasshoppers to devour crops, or send plagues among you. Then if my people who are called by my name will humble themselves and pray and seek my face and turn from their wicked ways, I will listen from heaven and will forgive their sins and restore their land."

It had taken twenty years to build what soon became known as "Solomon's Temple" and the wisdom of Solomon was gaining fame.

When the queen of Sheba heard of Solomon's fame and wisdom, she came to Jerusalem to test him with some hard questions. When she met with Solomon, she talked about everything that was on her mind. Solomon answered all her questions and explained many things to her.

Sheba realized how wise Solomon, and she gave the king a gift of 9,000 pounds of gold, great quantities of spices, and precious jewels.

Solomon ruled in Jerusalem over all Israel for forty years. When he died, he was buried in the City of David, named for his father. Then his son, Rehoboam became the next king.

Solomon wrote the thirty-one chapters in the Book of Proverbs in your Bible. Only by reading the Book of Proverbs will you realize the wisdom Solomon possessed!

[10]

RUTH

In the days when the judges ruled in Israel, a severe famine came upon the land. A man from Bethlehem in Judah left his home and went to live in the country of Moab, taking his wife and two sons with him. The man's name was Elimelech, and his wife was Naomi. Their two sons were Mahlon and Kilion. They were Ephrathites from Bethlehem in land of Judah. And when they reached Moab, they settled there.

Then Elimelech died, and left Naomi with their two sons. Soon the boys became older and married Moabite women. The oldest married a lady named Orpah, and the other married a lady named Ruth.

Ten years later Mahlon and Kilion both died in the same year; this left Naomi and her two daughters-in-law with no one to support them.

In order to survive Naomi decided to return to Bethlehem where members of her family lived.

She began the trip back home and Orpah and Ruth followed her. At their first stop on the journey, Naomi said to her daughters-in-law.

"Go back to your mothers' homes. And may the Lord reward you for the kindness to your husbands and to me. May the Lord bless you with the security of another marriage!" Then she kissed them good-bye and they all broke down and wept.

"No!" they said, "We want to go with you to your people." But, Naomi replied, "I've been away from my family these many years and have lost track of who is still alive. There's no future for you in Israel!" Again, they wept together, and Orpah kissed her mother-in-law good-bye. But Ruth clung tightly to Naomi.

"Look," Naomi said, "Your sister-in-law has gone back to her parents. You should do the same!" But Ruth replied, "Please don't ask me to leave you and turn back. Wherever you go, I will go, wherever you live I will live. Your people will be my people and your God will be my God. Wherever you die, I will die and there I will be buried. May the Lord punish me severely, if I allow anything but death to separate us!"

So, the two continued on their journey to Bethlehem. As they arrived in Bethlehem a cousin saw them arrive and ran out to greet them. "Naomi? Is that really you? I never thought I would see you again. There's only me left of our family, all the others have died, and I have wished I had died too. It is very hard to find enough work in order to survive. Who have you brought with you?" "This is Ruth," she said, "The widow of my son, Kilion and now your cousin."

Now there was a wealthy and influential man in Bethlehem named Boaz who was a relative of Naomi's husband Elimelech. "How are we going to make a living, to have enough bread to eat?" Ruth asked. "I'm able to labor in the fields, if anyone will hire me."

And as it happened, she found work in a field that was owned by Boaz. As Boaz inspected the field each day, he called to his foreman, "Who is that young woman over there? Who does she belong to?" And the foreman replied, "She is a young woman from Moab, who came back to Bethlehem with the widow of a relative of yours. She asked me this morning if she could gather grain behind the harvesters. She has been hard at work ever since, except for a few minutes rest in the shelter."

Boaz went over to Ruth and said, "I have been told that you are the daughter-in-law of my cousin's wife Naomi. Is this true?" "Yes. She replied. "I've ordered my foreman to give you a better paying job."

Ruth fell at his feet and thanked him warmly. "What have I done to deserve such kindness?" she said, "I am only a foreigner." "Yes, I know," Boaz replied. "I also know about everything you have done for your mother-in-law, since the death of your husband. I have heard how you left your father and mother and your own land to live here among complete strangers, and support your mother-in-law, since she is unable to support herself. You may work for me for as long as you wish, and I invite you and Naomi to dine with me tonight, it's lonely eating alone."

Ruth rushed home to tell Naomi of the good news! After they finished eating that evening, Boaz ask them to spend the night, because he wanted the discuss a subject the next day. Now in those days it was the custom in Israel: if a woman's husband died before they had children, that the man closest of kin and single should marry her, this way she can have a son to carry forward the family name. Boaz took Ruth into his home, and she became his wife. When he had slept with her, she became pregnant, and she gave birth to a son.

[11]

DANIEL

During the third year of King Jehoiakim's reign in Judah, King Nebuchadnezzar of Babylon came to Jerusalem and besieged it. The Lord gave him victory over King Jehoiakim of Judah and permitted him to take some of the sacred objects from the Temple of God. So, Nebuchadnezzar took them back to the Land of Babylonia and placed them in the treasure-house of his god. He also brought the young men from Jerusalem as captives, to be trained in the language and literature of Babylon.

Nebuchadnezzar ordered his chief of staff, Ashpenaz to select from the captives four to serve in his palace. "Make sure," he ordered, "That the ones you choose are strong, healthy, and good-looking young men. Make sure they are well versed in every branch of learning, are gifted with knowledge and good judgement, and are suited to serve in the royal palace!"

The ones selected would be given a daily ration of food and wine from the king's own kitchens. They were to be trained for three years, then they would enter the palace service.

Daniel, Hananiah, Mishael, and Azariah were four of the young chosen, all from the tribe of Judah. The food and wine in their diet was the finest in Babylon but contained many items of food the people of Israel had to avoid. Daniel was determined not to defile himself and refused to eat them. He asks the chief of staff for permission not to eat these unacceptable foods. He responded. "I command you and the others to eat this food and wine! It was the king's order to feed you this diet. I have seen King Nebuchadnezzar's anger when his orders are not followed; he has people killed and often puts them in the lion's den to be eaten. If you refuse to eat this food, you may become pale and thin compared to the other youths your age, I am afraid if the king learns of this I will be killed!"

Daniel spoke to the attendant who had been appointed to watch them eat, "Please test us for ten days on a diet of vegetables and water. At the end of this test the attendant saw for himself that Daniel and his three friends looked healthier and better nourished than the ones who ate the food assigned by the king.

God gave these four young men an unusual aptitude for understanding every aspect of literature and wisdom. And God gave Daniel the special ability to interpret the meanings of visions and dreams.

When the training period ordered by the king was completed, the chief of staff brought all the young men to King Nebuchadnezzar. The king talked to them all, but no one impressed him as much as Daniel. Whenever the king consulted Daniel on matters requiring wisdom and balanced judgment, he found Daniel ten times more capable than the others.

One night the king had such disturbing dreams that he could not sleep. He called his magicians, enchanters, sorcerers and astrologers, and commanded that they tell him what he had dreamed and the meaning of it. They agreed the king had asked them the impossible. The king became furious and ordered Arioch, the commander of the king's guard to kill them all, including Daniel.

When Arioch came to kill Daniel, he handled the situation with wisdom and discretion. Daniel asked Arioch, "Why has the king issued such a harsh decree?" Arioch told Daniel what had happened. Daniel asks Arioch, "Take me to the king before you kill me and I will give him the answers he seeks!" It being late in the evening, Arioch told him, "I will take you to the king tomorrow morning. I am leaving four of my men here with you so you can't escape!"

That night Daniel prayed to the God of heaven to reveal to him the dreams the king had dreamed and what were their meanings. That night the secret was revealed to Daniel in a vision.

The next morning Arioch took Daniel to King Nebuchadnezzar and said, " I have brought to you Daniel, one of the captives from Judah who will tell you the meaning of your dreams."

"Is this true Daniel? Can you tell me what my dream was and what it means?" "Your Majesty," Daniel replied, "while you were sleeping you dreamed about coming events, and it's not because I am wiser than anyone else that I know the secret of your dream but because my God wants you to understand what was in your heart"

"In your vision you saw standing before you a huge shining statue of a man. It was a frightening sight. The head of the statue was made of fine gold, its chest and arms were silver, its belly and thighs were bronze, its legs were iron, and its feet were a combination of iron and baked clay. As you watched a rock was cut from the mountain, but not by human hands. It struck the feet of iron and clay, smashing them to bits. Then the wind blew them away without a trace. The rock that knocked the statue down became a great mountain that covered the whole earth. That was your dream. Do you still want the meaning of this dream?" "Yes," the king told Daniel, "That was my dream, now I remember it. Now tell me what it means."

"Your Majesty" Daniel said, "You are the greatest of kings. The God of heaven has given you sovereignty, power, strength and honor. He has made you the ruler over all the inhabited world. You are the head of gold. But after your kingdom comes to an end, another kingdom inferior to yours, will rise to take your place. After that kingdom has fallen, yet a third kingdom represented by bronze, will rise to rule the world. Following that kingdom, there will be a fourth one as strong as iron. That kingdom will, smash and crush all previous empires. The feet and toes you saw were a combination of iron and baked clay. This shows in latter days there will be divisions among the people on earth. My God was showing you what is going to happen in the future." Then Daniel asks the king to cancel his decree that all the wise men in Babylon be executed.

Then the king gave Daniel many valuable gifts, as well as appointed him chief over all the wise men.

Now this is not the end of the story, there is a lot more to be told as a problem is created.

King Nebuchadnezzar had his skilled craftsmen create a golden statue ninety feet tall and nine feet wide and set it up on the plain of Dura in the province of Babylon. Then he sends messages to the governors, high officers, officials, advisers, treasurers, judges, magistrates, and others to come to the dedication of the statue he had set up. All these people came and stood before the statue he had set up.

Then a herald shouted out, "People of all races, nations, and languages, listen to the king's command! When you hear the horn, flute, zither, lyre, harp, pipes, and other musical instruments, bow to the ground to worship King Nebuchadnezzar's gold statue. Anyone who refuses to obey will immediately be thrown into a blazing furnace."

You must read for yourselves in the Book of Daniel, Chapter three to see what happens to them.

Then in Chapter four the king has another dream about a tree. Daniel is called to explain this dream. Here too, you must read for yourself the explanation of this dream.

To finish the story of Daniel life, there is a lot more to tell: The writing on the wall, Daniel is put in the lion's den, the angel of the Lord, Gabriel, visits

Daniel, and then a visit from the archangel Michael. At the end of the Book of Daniel he is told, "Go your way until the end. You will rest, then at the end of the days, you will rise again to receive the inheritance set aside for you."

[12]

PAUL

When Jesus Christ began His ministry on earth, His mission was to call the Israelites back to worshipping God because they had strayed away and were worshipping other gods. They were under Roman rule and owned no land of their own.

The Pharisees and Sadducees often went to the Jordan River to witness the call of John the Baptist to repent of their sins (little did they know that John was just paving the way for Jesus).

John often reminds the crowd that followed him that he baptized with water, but there one coming soon, greater than he, that would best the crowds in a different way!

The teachings of Jesus (the best of these, The Sermon on the mountain), and the miracles and healing of the sick was causing people to leave the Pharisees and Sadducees and become a Christian.

Saul was a Pharisee who hated the Christian movement that was becoming popular with the people. He agreed that something had to be done.

We know very little of Saul's early life: His parents were Gamalians. There is no record of their name, nor is there any reference in the Bible if he had brother or sisters. All we know is he was a Citizen of Rome, a Jew, a very educated man, and hated what Jesus was doing. He knew it had to be stopped! Saul was a Zealous persecutor and took every opportunity to have the followers of Jesus killed.

Stephen was a deacon in Jerusalem in the first year of Christianity. He appealed to the Sanhedrin (high council of the synagogue).

"You stubborn people! You are heathen at heart and deaf to the truth. Must you forever resist the Holy Spirit? You can't name a prophet your ancestors didn't persecute and kill!"

Saul was one of the witnesses to Stephen remarks. He agreed Stephen had to be killed (Acts 8:1), and witnessed the stoning of his death. Saul was going everywhere to destroy Christians. He went from house to house, dragging out both men and women who were followers of Jesus and putting them in prison.

Saul went to the high priest and received a letter addressed to the synagogues in Damascus, asking for their cooperation in the arrest of Christians (often called Nazarenes), he wanted to bring them back to Jerusalem in chains.

What happen to Saul on the road to Damascus, you must read for yourself (Acts 9)!

Soon the people heard Paul (Saul becomes a new Christian with a new name) preaching about Jesus in the synagogues.

All who heard were amazed, "Isn't this the same man who caused such devastation among the followers of Jesus in Jerusalem?"

Paul's preaching became more and more powerful, as he continued to tell others of his experience as he traveled to Damascus.

Paul returned to his home in Jerusalem and tried to meet with the believers, but was refused fellowship with them, as they had witnessed his goal in Jerusalem, and his part in the death of Stephen. They were afraid of him!

Paul met Barnabas, who was a Hellenized Jew who joined the Jerusalem church soon after Christ's crucifixion. Barnabas was one of the Cypriots who founded the church at Antioch.

They became very close friends, and as brothers in Christ, often preached and traveled together. Barnabas was close to the Apostles still living in Jerusalem who Paul wanted to meet and learn first-hand of their experience while traveling with the Messiah!

Paul returned to the church in Antioch, often preaching there when Barnabas went to start new churches. It was here in Antioch that the believers were first called "Christians".

Paul became probably the greatest evangelist to ever live in my opinion (he carried "the word" throughout the world --before Billy Graham). To learn more on Paul. Start reading about his first missionary journey in the 13th chapter in the Book of Acts!

Paul wrote the Book of Romans, First and Second Corinthians, Galatians, Ephesians, Philippians, Colossians, First and Second Thessalonians, First and Second Timothy, Titus, and Philemon.

At the start of this Chapter, I did mention that Paul was very educated — this is shown in these books written by him, his skill in the writing of these letters!

The exact details of St. Paul's death are unknown, but tradition holds that he was beheaded in Rome and thus died as a martyr for his faith.

His death was perhaps part of the execution of Christians ordered by the Roman emperor Nero.

[13]

THE TWELVE

After Jesus was baptized by John, Jesus was led by the Spirit into the wilderness to be tempted by Satan. When Jesus heard that John had been arrested, he left Judea and returned to Galilee.

He went first to Nazareth, then left there and moved to Capernaum, beside the Sea of Galilee, in the region of Zebulun and Naphtali. This fulfilled what God said through the prophet Isaiah (read in Matthew 4:15-16). From then on Jesus began to preach. "Repent of your sins and turn to God, for the kingdom of heaven is near."

Jesus chooses twelve men to be his disciples: Peter, John, James, Andrew, Philip, Thomas, Bartholomew, Matthew, James (son of Alphacus), Simon (the Zealot), Judas (son of James), and Judas.

Peter exhibits the character of an outspoken leader of the disciples, willing to challenge Jesus' actions and teachings (John 13:6). Although quick to commit to Jesus' challenges (John 13:9), he is unsteady in demonstrating his commitment during Jesus' time of suffering (John 18:15,25). Roman Catholic tradition holds St. Peter as the first pope (Matthew 16:19), which is why he is often depicted at the gates of heaven in art and popular culture.

The Bible does not tell us how Peter died. The most accepted was that he was crucified upside down (by his own request).

John is my favorite of the twelve; not only being referred to as "the one whom Jesus loved", he was the last of the twelve to die. He wrote the Gospel of John, the epistles: John, 2nd and 3rd John and the book of Revelation. John and his brother James were sons of Zebedee, and they along with Peter witnessed the Transfiguration.

It was for his witnessing for Jesus that he had been sentenced to hard labor on an island. There, God sent an angel to tell John the things that were going to happen in the future. In Revelation 1:3, read it for yourself (see what is in store for those who read this prophecy).

James, son of Zebedee, became the chief spokes-
man of the Jerusalem church, as Peter fled from Jerusalem to save his life. (Acts 12:1-17)

He was distinguished as being in Jesus' innermost
circle and the only apostle whose martyrdom is recorded in the bible (Acts 12:2).

He framed his writing with an overall theme of
patient perseverance during trials and temptations.
James writes in order to encourage his readers to live
consistently with what they have learned in Christ.
He condemns various sins including pride, hypocrisy,
favoritism, and slander. He was killed with a sword
by the order of King Agrippa as he began to persecute the followers of Jesus.

Andrew was the older brother of Peter. He was
born in the village of Bethsaida on the sea of Galilee.
He and his brother were fisherman. It was Andrew
who told Peter "We have found the Messiah" and
brought him to meet Jesus.

Despite his seeming important role as an early follower of Christ, Andrew is only mentioned twelve
times in the entire New Testament —and four of
those times are simply as one of the Disciples. Andrew was sentenced to death by crucifixion in the
city of Patras.

Philip preached the gospel in Scythia (a region in
central Eurasia), Syria, and Phrygia (Turkey).

Church tradition holds that he was one of the churches most valuable missionaries.

There is not much about Philip from the synoptic gospels or Book of Acts, in fact, pretty much all we learn is that he is listed with Bartholomew.

My thought is that the two of them traveled together because it was the custom at the time that missionaries always traveled in pairs!

Bartholomew is listed among the twelve apostles of Jesus in the synoptic gospels: Matthew, Mark, and Acts (Matthew 3:16-19, Mark 6;14-16, Luke 6:14-16, Acts 1:13). He was one of the witnesses of the ascension of Jesus.

There is no record of his role in the formation of the early church. It is unknown if he ever preached, traveled as a missionary, or used any of the powers he possessed given to him by Jesus. It is not recorded in the bible how he was called to be one of the twelve. I am sure he was present at the Sermon on the Mount, as well as when the multitudes were fed, and he is always in the picture of the Last Supper!

Thomas was probably born in Galilee to a humble family, there is no indications that he was a fisherman. He was a Jew, but there is no account of how he became an apostle to Christ.

Thomas is famous for having doubted the resurrection of Jesus and demanded physical proof of the wounds of Christ crucifixion. The phrase "doubting Thomas" was coined for his lack of faith. Another lack of faith was shown by John the Baptist, when he sent his disciples to inquire of Jesus, "Are you the Messiah?"

Jesus told Thomas after the physical examination, "Now you believe, but blessed are they that have not seem me. and yet have believed!"

Few Christians realize there is a Book:

Gospel of Thomas and is actively use by the Catholic Church. The early church father failed to canonize this writing because it was grounded in Gnosticism, the philosophical and religious movement of the 2nd century.

Matthew was called by Jesus to follow him. At that time he was a tax collector, one of the most reviled professions in ancient Judaism. Because of his occupation, it is thought he would have been very educated, knowing how to read and write and speak in several languages, and he also knew arithmetic. His book became the most important of all Gospel texts for first and second century Christians because it contains all the elements important to the early church: the story about Jesus' miraculous conception; an explanation of the importance of liturgy, law, discipleship, and teachings and an account of the life of Jesus. He was arrested in Ethiopia and probably this was the place of his death.

James the son of Alphaeus. There are two men named James in the bible. I often get confused on which was which. Scholars disagree on which of the two wrote the Book of James. When Jesus died on the cross, all four gospels say there was a woman named Mary there who was "the mother of James", and Mark 15:40 clarifies it was this James.

I will not say more, because I just don't know. Only thing I am sure of is that they were both disciples of Christ!

Simon the Zealot is one of the most obscure apostles. He plays no particular role in the beginning of Christianly. It is thought he may have preached in Egypt, then joined the apostle Judas in Persia, where according to the apocryphal where he was martyred by being cut in half with a saw.

Judas was a brother of Jesus (Matthew 13:55. Mark 6:3), and the writer of the Epistle of Jude. He was also known as Thaddaeus.

Mark 6:3 Tells us that Jesus had four younger brothers and at least two sisters. The brothers were: James, Joses, Simon and Judas. The sisters' names have not been preserved.

According to some tradition, Salome was a sister of Mary, Jesus' mother, making Salome the aunt of Jesus, and her sons would then be cousins of Jesus. It is very likely that one of Jesus' sisters was named Salome, as was the custom at that time. Also, you are most likely aware that Jesus and John the Baptist were cousins.

Judas Iscariot is notorious for betraying Jesus!

As he traveled with the other eleven, he was the most trusted, and all money collected was given to him. Scholars cannot agree when Satan took over his life.

Jesus tells in Matthew 26:24 how terrible it will be for one who betrays him. "It would have been far better for that man if he had never been born!"

At the Passover meal as Jesus washed his feet, I wonder the thoughts of Judas at that time? The bible tells us (Matthew 27:3-40, when Judas realized that Jesus had been condemned to die, he was filled with remorse. He returned the thirty pieces of silver and declared to them that he had betrayed an innocent man. He then went and hanged himself; but in Acts, Luke tells a different ending. Read for yourself if you are interested in learning the way Luke says he died in Acts 2:18-19.

Peter tells how in the book of Psalm it tells them they should select a person to replace Judas.

So, they nominated two men: Barsabbas and Matthias. Then the 120 who were in attendance prayed and voted which of these two who would be the new Apostle. Matthias was selected to serve with the other eleven.

Matthias was chosen from among Jesus' disciples to replace Judas as to complete the twelve.

After receiving the Holy Spirit on the day of Pentecost and hearing Paul preach and 3,000 come forward to receive Christ as their Savior, he left to preach in Judah and Colchis where he was crucified.

[14]

NOAH

God observed the extent of human wickedness that had come upon the earth in the generations following Adam and Eve being expelled from the Garden of Eden, (just a note, you should read the book Paradise Lost written by John Melton in 1667). God saw everything the people were doing was consistently and totally evil.

So, the Lord was sorry He had ever made mankind and put them on earth; observing how corrupt the world had become the Lord said, "I will wipe this human race I have created from the face of the earth. Yes, and I will destroy every living thing —all the people, animals (at this time there were giant Nephilites). Even the birds of the sky will die." Was all this sinning in the world a result of the people's long life spans? Methuselah had lived 969 years. God was going to destroy everything, but one man, Noah, found favor with the Lord.

Noah was a righteous man; he and his family were the only blameless persons on earth. God told Noah to build the Ark. When the Ark was finished the Lord told Noah to bring a pair of every kind of animal, male and female, into the boat, to leave behind the giant Nephilites, also bring pairs of every kind of bird. God told Noah, "In the future the lifespan of humans will be no more than 120 years."

The years Noah was building the Ark, he had been the joke of the people. They were laughing at him daily or saying other harsh words. There had never been rain before! I guess Noah got the last laugh as drops of water began to fall from the sky. After water covered the earth, the flood recedes and after 150 days, exactly five months from the time the flood began, the Ark came to rest on the mountain of Ararat.

When it was possible for Noah and his family to leave the Ark do you know the first thing he did? If you want to know read in your bible Genesis 8:18-22.

God rewarded Noah for his righteousness and obedience, saving both him and his family from destruction.

Noah's parents father was Lamech, and his children were Shem, Japheth, and Ham. His grandchildren were Cush, Aram, Canaan, Magog, Lud, Put, and more.

Noah was ninth is descent from Adam. And grandson of Methuselah. He died at the age of 950 years.

The story of the flood demonstrations both the gravity of God's justice and the promise of His salvation! God made a covenant with Noah and told him, "I have placed my rainbow in the clouds. It is the sign of my covenant with you that I will never again destroy the earth with water."

As we see the rainbow in the clouds today, we should all remember why it is there.

[15]

STEPHEN

As the number of believers rapidly multiplied, there were rumblings of discontent. The Greek speaking believers complained about the Hebrew speaking believers, saying that their widows were being discriminated against in the daily distribution of food.

These complaints and accusations had been going on for a long time. Constantly, an apostle was called to try bringing peace to the group. Soon the apostles spent all their time settling this dispute!

Finally, one of the apostles (we don't which one), came up with a plan. They would select a committee of seven people to handle this problem and said, "We apostles should spend our time teaching and preaching the word of God, not running a food program".

This plan was well accepted by both Greek and Hebrew. The seven selected were: Stephen, Philip, Procorus, Nicanor, Timon, Parmenas and Nicolas. These seven were ordained as deacons and they were to oversee this program.

Stephen was a Hellenist Jew, loud spoken, and full of the Spirit of God (one might say, a natural-born leader). He was full of God's Grace and power and performed amazing miracles and signs among the people.

But one day some men from the Synagogue of Freed Slaves, as it was called, started to debate with him. They were Jews from Cyrene, Alexander, Cilicia and the province of Asia.

None of them could stand against the wisdom and Spirit with which Stephen spoke; so, they persuaded some men to lie about him telling they had heard Stephen blaspheme Moses. Stephen was arrested and brought before the high council. The liars testified to the council, "We have heard him say that this Jesus of Nazareth will destroy the Temple and change the customs Moses handed down to us."

At this point everyone in the high council stared at Stephen, because his face became as bright as an angel's. Then the high priest asked, "Are these accusations true." At this Stephen addresses the council.

If you want to know what Stephen said, read It for yourself: Chapter seven in the Book of Acts. Stephen's speech lays a firm ideological foundation for the subsequent movement of the focus of God's Word.

Stephens most effective contribution to the kingdom of God comes through his martyrdom. It may be God's will for our life is not one that takes us from blessing to blessing, but rather one that follows Stephen on the road to martyrdom!

As Stephen was being stoned to death his last words were, "Lord, do not hold this sin against them." He died as Paul watched!

[16]

SAMSON

The Israelites did evil in the Lord's sight, so the Lord handed them over to the Philistines, who oppressed them for forty years.

In those days a man named Manoah from the tribe of Dan lived in the town of Zorah. His wife was unable to become pregnant and they had no children. The angel of the Lord appeared to Manoah's wife and said, "Even though you have been unable to have children, you will become pregnant and give birth to a son, and his hair must never be cut. For he will be dedicated to God as a Nazirite from birth. He is the chosen one who will rescue Israel from the Philistines." The woman ran to tell her husband the good news.

When her son was born, she named him Samson. And the Lord blessed him as he grew up.

One day when Samson was in Timnah, one of the Philistine women caught his eye (Oops! There's going to be trouble soon). When Samson got home he told his father and mother, "A young Philistine woman in Timnah caught my eye, I want to marry her. Get her for me."

His father and mother objected. "Why would you want to marry a Philistine woman, there are many single women in Israel who haven't been promised, beautiful ones too!" But Samson told his father, "Get her for me! She looks good to me."

His father and mother did not realize the Lord was at work in this, creating an opportunity to work against the Philistines.

As Samson and his parents were going down to Timnah to find the young lady Samson had seen and talk to her parents, a young lion suddenly attacked Samson near the vineyards of Timnah. At that moment the Spirit of the Lord came powerfully upon him and he ripped the lion's jaws apart with his bare hands.

Arrangements were made for him to marry Delilah. A couple of weeks later as Samson returned to Timnah for the wedding he traveled the same path. He passed the lion he had killed and noticed in the carcass a swarm of bees making honey. Samson had a bachelor's party. There was a custom for the bride's parents to select several men to be the grooms assistants. During the party there was a lot of wine being consumed. Samson said to all at the party, "Let me tell you a riddle. If you solve my riddle during these seven days of celebration, I will buy each of you a fine robe, but if you can't solve it, then each of you must buy me the same." "All right," they agreed, "let's hear your riddle." Samson said the riddle is this, "Out of the one who eats came something to eat: out of the strong came something sweet." Three days later they were still trying to figure it out. On the fourth day they asked Delilah to ask Samson the answer to the riddle. So, Delilah came to Samson with tears in her eyes and said, "You don't love me; you hate me! You have given my friends a riddle, but you haven't told me the answer." Samson replied, "I haven't even given my parents the answer. Why should I tell you?" She cried for the next three days and constantly begged Samson to give her the answer to the riddle.

On the last day of the celebration Samson gave Delilah the answer to the riddle. At the close of the celebration the men came to Samson and said, "This is our answer to your riddle. "What is sweeter than honey? What is stronger than a lion?" "If you hadn't got the answer from my bride, you wouldn't have been able to solve my riddle," he answered. To pay the wager to the men; Samson went down to the town of Ashkelon and killed men and took their robes to settle the debt. Samson was furious at Delilah and returned home to live with his parents. So as the story goes, Delilah was given in marriage to Samson's best man at the wedding. Weeks later Samson cooled off from the betrayal of his bride and returned to marry her (not being aware she had been given to another). Delilah's father explained the situation to him, and offered him Delilah's younger sister, who was more beautiful to marry. Then he hated the Philistines as much as his parents. To learn more on Samson's vengeance on the Philistines you must read for yourself in the Book of Judges Chapter 15.

Finally, the Philistines captured Samson as he was spending the night with a prostitute. Some time later Samson fell in love with another woman named Delilah. She betrayed him too by telling the Philistines the source of his strength. This immense physical strength was used against the Philistines for over twenty years.

[17]

ELIJAH

Now Elijah, who was from Tishbe in Gilead, told King Ahab, who had lost two sons because he attempted to rebuild Jericho, "As surely as the Lord, the God of Israel lives —The God I serve —there will be no dew or rain during the next few years until I give the word!"

Then the Lord said to Elijah, "Go to the east and hide by Kerith Brook, near where it enters the Jordan River. Drink from the brook and eat what the ravens bring you, for I have commanded them to bring you food." Elijah did as the Lord told him. Soon the brook dried up, for there was no rain anywhere in the land.

Then the Lord said to Elijah, "Go and live in the village of Zarephath near the city of Sidon. I have instructed a widow there to feed you." So he went to

Zarephath. As he arrived at the gates of the village, he saw a widow gathering sticks, and he asked her, "Would you please bring me a little water in a cup?" As she was going to get it, he called to her, "Bring me a bite of bread too."

But she said, "I swear by the Lord, your God that I don't have a single piece of bread in the house. And I have only a handful of flour left in the jar and a little cooking oil in the bottom of the jug. I was just gathering a few sticks to cook this last meal, and then my son and I will die."

But Elijah said to her, "Don't be afraid! Go ahead and do just what you've said but make a little bread for me first. Then use what's left to prepare a meal for yourself and your son. For this is what the Lord, the God of Israel, says: There will always be flour and olive oil left in your containers until the time when the Lord sends rain and the crops grow again!"

King Ahab had offered large sums of money to anyone who would tell him where Elijah was hiding; he wanted to kill him for stopping the rain, as many of his people were starving to death.

Later, in the third year of the drought, the Lord said to Elijah, "Go present yourself to King Ahab, tell him I will soon send rain!"

When King Ahab saw Elijah, he ordered his guard to seize him and bring him to the palace. "So, this is the troublemaker of Israel, that cursed the land with no rain all these years, causing many to die."

"I have made no trouble for Israel," Elijah replied, "It is you and your family who are the troublemakers! For you have refused to obey the commands of the Lord and have worshiped the images of Baal instead." Elijah told the King, "I am the only prophet of the Lord's that's left, but Baal has 450 prophets. Let us have a test to determine which the people of Israel will serve," and Baal's prophets agreed!

To learn more of this test, you must read it for yourself! Start reading in your Bible at 1st Kings Chapter 18:22-46. (Actually, you should read from there through Chapter 22)!

After King Ahab's death, the land of Moab rebelled against Israel. The new king, Ahaziah, fell through the latticework in the palace and was seriously injured. He could hardly move or speak. King Ahaziah realized he might not survive, so he sent messengers to the temple of Baal-zebub seeking the answer if he would recover. Shortly the messengers returned, and the king enquired the answer they had received. They replied, "A man came up to us and told us to go back to our king and give him this message, 'This is what the Lord says: Is there no God in Israel? Why are you sending men to Baal-zebub, the god of Ekron, to ask, whether you will recover?

Therefore, because you have done this, you will never leave the bed you are lying on, you will surely die.'"

"What sort of man was he?' the king demanded. "What did he look like?" They replied, "He was a hairy man, and he wore a leather belt around his waist."

"Elijah from Tishbe!' The king exclaimed. The king sent a captain of his guard with fifty men to arrest him.

To prove he was a man of God, Elijah killed the men with fire from heaven. The second time the king sent men for the same purpose. Again, they were consumed by fire. On the third attempt Elijah agreed to go to the king. There's more to this story if you will read chapter two in the 2nd Book of Kings.

Elijah was carried to heaven in a chariot of fire. Note: the first person to enter heaven without dying was Enoch, as he was carried up in a whirlwind.

Elijah was a mighty prophet during a turbulent time in Israel's history. The nation had turned away from the Lord to worship Baal and King Ahab had formed an alliance with Sidon by marrying their princess, Jezebel. Elijah was sent to show Israel the evil of their ways and encourage them to return to the Lord.

[18]

MARY MAGDALENE

There is no person in history that is as controversial or mysterious as Mary Magdalene. A devoted follower of Jesus, Mary followed him to the very end and was the first to witness His resurrection. Since then, she has been labeled such things as a prostitute, Jesus' wife, an apostle and writer of the Gnostic Gospel of Mary. Her name has been cleared of being a prostitute; yet she and her life are still heavily studied and strongly debated.

Mary's appearances are few in the Bible, mostly in the days surrounding Easter weekend, but her actions and the effort to identify her have made her into a major figure in Christianity.

Mary is first mentioned (Luke 8:3) as one of the followers of Jesus in whom He had cast out seven demons. In the Gospel of Philip, Mary is referred to as Jesus' companion, who He loved very much (even more than John?).

Some wish the ceremony that celebrates the beginning of an alleged marriage of Jesus and Mary to be viewed as a holy wedding, and their alleged daughter, Sarah, to be viewed as a holy family in order to question traditional gender roles and family values.

Christian tradition has long held that Jesus was not married, even when no evidence exists to support this claim! The debate over this issue brought many theologians against each other when in 2003 the book, The Da Vinci Code written by Dan Brown, became one of the best sellers!

Only one other thing I will say about this is that a previous unknown scrap of ancient papyrus contains the words, "Jesus said to them, my wife."

There are so many Marys in the Bible, it is hard for me to keep straight which is which as Mary was the most common name for a Jewish woman.

She was from the fishing town of Magdala, on the western shore of the Sea of Galilee. Her family was wealthy, but Mary had more problems than most people. Satan tried every way he could to keep her under his control (seven demons in her, a severe medical problem and who knows what else Satan threw her way).

There is so much more that could be said about Mary Magdalene. I find it hard to find a stopping place. I suggest you read for yourself the story of this amazing lady.

One thing is certain about Mary Magdalene, she holds a special place in the story of Christianity and was placed there by God!

[19]

TIMOTHY

There is only one mention of Lois and Eunice in the bible. They were the grandmother and the mother of Paul's young protege, Timothy.

Timothy was raised with such a devout and fervent faith by these two! Eunice was a Jewish believer who had been married to a Greek man, which would explain the fact that as an infant, Timothy was not circumcised as all Jewish boys were.

Lois was either Eunice's mother or her mother-in-law. The fact that she helped rear Timothy may indicate that Timothy's father had died or that the family all lived together, which was not uncommon in those days. It is possible that the father had died while Timothy was young since Paul takes on a fatherly role with Timothy and often refers to him as "my true son in the faith." Timothy's godly upbringing is referenced many times though out the New Testament. From the days he was a child, he had been taught the sacred writing, Jewish traditions, and other things including the story of salvation which gave him wisdom of Christianity in his early teens!

Timothy had come a long way in the year or two since his conversion to Christ. He had a lot more to learn as he left Lystra and Iconium, headed west with Paul and Silas to evangelize the lost. His youthfulness and good looks helped attracted the younger generation into Christianity!

Timothy was filled with the Holy Spirit and soon he was evangelizing on his own.

Paul writes to him often encouraging him. In 2nd Timothy Paul says, "Never be ashamed to tell others about our Lord." In Paul's first letter to him (chapter 5) Timothy is told, "Never speak harshly to an older man, but appeal to him respectfully as you would to your own father. Talk to younger men as you would to your own brother. Treat older women as you would your own mother and treat younger women as you would treat your own sisters!" Paul tells him (1st Timothy 6:23), "Don't drink only water. You ought to drink a little wine for the sake of your stomach because you are sick so often." There's no evidence to support my theory, but I suspect Timothy wrote to Paul often too.

Saint Timothy is the patron saint of stomach and intestinal aliments owing it to Saint Paul's advice.

[20]

SATAN

I feel very qualified to write about Satan! Though he is much older than me: I know him personally! He makes me say things, I regret saying, gives me thoughts I should not have in my mind, and tells me many lies trying to make me think they are true.

It is only by the grace of God, and having the Holy Spirit come into me when I confessed my sins to Jesus, and ask Him to forgive me that I can thank Him for shedding His blood for my sins and follow in His steps, and do His will!

There is more about Satan in the Bible, than any other figure. He claimed his first and greatest victory in the Garden of Eden, when he started "SIN".

Before he made his debut on earth, he was an Angel in heaven. In the council in heaven Lucifer, as Satan was then called, rebelled against God. Since that time, he has sought to destroy the children of God on the earth and to make them miserable!

One primary issue in the conflict between God and Satan is the problem of agency. Agency is a precious gift from God; it is essential to His plan for His children. In Satan's rebellion against God, Satan "sought to destroy the agency of man". God said, "I will redeem all mankind, that one shall not be lost, and surely I will do it; wherefore give me thine honor."

God allows Satan and Satan's followers to tempt us as part of our experience in mortality. Because Satan "seeth that all men might be miserable like unto himself". He directs his most strenuous opposition at righteousness. He attacks the most important aspects of the Heavenly Father's plan of happiness. For example, he seeks to discredit the Savior and the priesthood, to cast doubt on the power of the Savior and to counterfeit revelation, to distract us from the truth, and to contradict individual accountability. He attempts to undermine the family by confusing gender, promoting sexual relations outside of marriage, ridiculing marriage, and discouraging childbearing by married adults who would otherwise raise children in righteousness.

In his rebellion, he and his followers were cast out of heaven. They were cut off from God and were unable to have a physical body.

So that you may start to understand the role of Satan in the Bible, I suggest you read the book, Satan Is Alive And Doing Well On The Planet Earth by Hal Lindsey (author of the book Late Great Planet Earth). This book outlines the "battle plan" Satan will use to destroy Christianly.

Holiness can change to evil in the blink of an eye. From the day each of us are born, until the day we die, we will spend eternity in hell, if during our life we fail to make the most important decision of our life!

The road to heaven is easy to follow; just read John 3:16 in your Bible "For God loved the world so much that he gave his one and only son, so that everyone who believes in him will not perish but have eternal life."

Satan and his followers had control of earth and its population for centuries without anyone challenging their authority! They had made it so evil that God considered destroying the whole creation and would have if it had not been for Noah.

Then things changed as God made a covenant with Abraham promising to protect him and that his descendants would be more than the number of grains of sand on a beach, or more numerous that stars in the sky. "How can this be Lord, for you have not given Sarah the ability to become pregnant." When Abraham told his wife the good news she laughed. "Why did she laugh?" the Lord said to Abraham, "and say 'Can an old woman like me have a baby?' Is anything too hard for the Lord? I will return about this time next year and Sarah will give birth to your son! Remember, you and all your descendants will have my protection if you worship me, and no other."

Here is the challenge, Satan, thought to himself, I will corrupt all of Abraham's descendants and get revenge for God casting me out of heaven. Satan called a staff meeting of the one-third of the angels that were cast down from heaven with him. "Our chance has come!" Satan told them. "We will fight, as we have never had to before, to corrupt these people who God thinks His protection will save. Go out in teams of two, search all over the earth where Abraham's descendants live, convince them with lies, untruths or by whatever means you can to create doubt about their relationship with God. Now follow me to the cities of Sodom and Gomorrah and I'll give you a lesson!"

As time passes, Satan's rule over earth goes unchallenged. He convinced Esau to sell his birthright for a bowl of soup, got Shechem to rape the daughter of Jacob and Leah, and made it possible for Joseph to bring all the Jews (Abraham's children) to Egypt where they become slaves.

After four hundred years of being slaves, crying and praying to God for deliverance, God answers their prayers.

Moses, one of the many who Satan has never been able to get to worship him or do his dirty work comes on the scene in this war on earth. To learn how Moses got Pharaoh to release the slaves, you must read for yourselves. (Exodus)

Satan shows his power. Shortly, after the Israelites have their freedom, Aaron is coaxed into making a statue of a golden calf and of the people began to worship it as their God. God was furious!

This warfare continues through the books of the Old Testament! It appears Satan is winning.

God thought to Himself, something must be done. He had sent many prophets to warn His people, only to have them killed by Satan's forces. "The only way to end this war is for me to go to earth myself and show my people how they are to live! I will become fully human as they are, laying my creatorship aside."

If you do not know the story of God's coming to earth, stop! The four Gospels contains this record.

Satan does not waste any time in getting word of His birth, and seeks for ways to kill the child! It never came to Satan's attention that God was going to win this battle. Satan failed to realize that John the Baptist (calling people to repent of their sins) was just paving the way for the ministry of Jesus.

After the Baptism of Jesus, Jesus was led by the Spirit to meet His enemy face to face. Three times Satan sought to get him to worship him, with no success!

Satan finds Saul, who will obey him completely. In Saul's own words. "I became very zealous to honor God. I persecuted the followers of the Way, hounding some to death, arresting both men and women throwing them into prison, I even held the coats of the men when they stoned Stephen to death." This is the type of person Satan loves! One who will do his work, no questions asked.

You can read the words of this prophecy on the way it will all end. Blessed is the one who reads the words of this prophecy to the church and He blesses all who listen to its message and obey what it says, for the time is near.

[21]

PSALMS

This book wouldn't be complete in my opinion if I did not mention the Book of Psalm.

David had a special way in praising God!

Psalm 1, "Oh, the joy of those who do not follow the advice of the wicked, or stand around with sinners, or join in with mockers. But their delight is in law of the Lord, meditating on it day and night —." That is the way it is!

David tells us what the Lord means to him in Psalms 23, "The Lord is my shepherd; I have all I need. — He guides me along right paths, bringing honor to his name—. My cup overflows with blessings."

Each morning, part of my prayers come from Psalm 25: 4-7 "Show me the right path, O Lord; point out the road for me to follow. Lead me by your truth and teach me, for you are the God who saves me. All day long I put my hope in you. Remember, O Lord your compassion and unfailing love, which you have shown from long ages past. Do not remember the rebellious sins of my youth. Remember me in the light of your

unfailing love."

Another part of my daily prayer is in Psalm 86:11-12 "Teach me your ways, O Lord, that I may live according to your truth! Grant me purity of heart, so that I may honor you. With all my heart I will praise you, O Lord my God. I will give glory to your name forever".

Again, in his praise, we are told by David the ways of God. Psalm 33:13-15 "The Lord looks down from heaven and sees the whole human race. From his throne he observes all who live on the earth. He made their hearts, so he understands everything they do.

Psalm 37:3-4 "Trust in the Lord and do good. Then you will live safely in the land and prosper. Take delight in the Lord, and he will give you your heart's desire."

Psalm 39:4-5 "Lord remind me how brief my time on earth will be. Remind me that my days are numbered — how fleeting my life is. You have made my life no longer than the width of my hand. My entire life is just a moment to you; at best each of us is but a breath."

Psalm 89:48 "No one can escape the power of the grave."

Two of my favorite passages in Psalm are Psalm 103:8-15 "The Lord is compassionate and merciful, slow to get angry and filled with unfailing love. He will not" — I encourage you to read verses 10-15. My favorite is Psalms 119:105 "Your word is a lamp to guide my feet and a light for my path."

[22]

LAST CHAPTER

As I come to the end of this writing of "Between The Lines", it is my desire that you have enjoyed the book. It is my hope that it has caused you to have opened your Bible.

Let me assure you, there is nothing in the Bible that is not important. It is there for a reason!

There are men and women who appear in only one line in the Old Testament and New Testament.

There are a few I will mention.

Anna (a prophet) was the daughter of Phanual from the tribe of Asher. In the seventh year of their marriage her husband died. She lived to be eighty-four. After becoming a widow, she stayed in the temple, day and night, worshiping God with fasting and prayer. She saw Jesus on the eighth day of his life as he was brought to the temple to be circumcised.

Simeon was a righteous and devoted man and was eagerly waiting for the Messiah to come and rescue Israel. The Holy Spirit had revealed to him that he would not die until he saw the Messiah. So as Mary and Joseph came to present the baby Jesus to the Lord as the law required. Simeon was there as they entered to temple. He took the child in his arms and praised God saying, "Sovereign Lord, now let your servant die in peace as you have promised. I have seen your salvation, which you have prepared for all people. He is a light to reveal God to the nations, and He is the glory of your people Israel."

Ananias and Sapphira where members of the early church and united in heart and mind that what they owned was not their own, so they shared everything they had. There were no needy people among them because those who owned land or houses would sell them and bring the money to the apostles to give to those in need. They sold some land and brought only a part of it to the Apostles, claiming it was the full amount. Then Peter said, "Ananias, why have you let Satan enter your heart? You lied to the Holy Spirit. How could you do a thing like this?"

As soon as Ananias heard these words, he fell to the floor and died. When Sapphira returned, Peter questioned her, "Did you and your husband give us the full price of the land you sold?"

"Yes," she replied, "that was the full amount." If you want to know what happened to her, read it for yourself. (Acts 5:10)

Cornelius was a devout, God-fearing man, as well as everyone in his household. This was unusual as he was a Roman Army Officer and the Captain of a Regiment in Caesarea.

One afternoon at about three o'clock, he had a vision in which he saw an angel of God coming toward him. "Cornelius!" the angel said. "What is it sir?" he asked the angel. "Your prayers, gifts to the poor, and the way you live has been noticed by God. God wants you to visit with Peter, who is staying with a tanner in Joppa. Send someone to ask him to come to Caesarea."

At this same time Peter had gone up on the flat roof of the house where he was staying to pray. It was about noon, and he was hungry. But while a meal was being prepared, he fell into a trance. He saw the sky open, and something like a large sheet was let down by its four corners. In the sheet were all sort of animals, reptiles, and birds. Then a voice said to him, "Get up Peter; kill and eat them."

"No, Lord," Peter declared. "I have never eaten anything that our Jewish laws have declared impure and unclean." But the voice spoke again, "Do not call something unclean if God has made it clean." This same vision was repeated three times. Then the sheet was suddenly pulled up to Heaven.

A few days later, the message from Cornelius was received asking Peter to come to Caesarea to preach to the people there and stay at his house.

When Peter arrived in Caesarea Cornelius was waiting for him, and as Peter arrived at his house he fell at his feet and worshipped him. Peter pulled him up and said, "Stand up! I'm a human being just like you!" So, they talked together and went inside, where many others were assembled.

As they were entering the house, Peter turned to Cornelius and said, "You know it is against our laws for a Jewish man to enter a Gentile home like this or to associate with you. I had a vision before your message reached me to come. The Lord told me this would happen, and that I should come and give you a message." If you want to know what the message was, you must read it for yourself. Most Christians consider Cornelius to be the first Gentile to convert to the faith!

Simon (from Cyrene) was the man compelled by the Romans to carry the cross of Jesus of Nazareth as Jesus was taken to his crucifixion.

It is unknown what happen to Simon after he carried the cross. He is not venerated as a saint, though it is hard to believe that being so close to Jesus would not have changed him!

There are fourteen men in the New Testament named Simon (here I had the same problem as with so many Marys).

Simon witnessed the death of Jesus, between two thieves: Gestas on his left and Dismus on his right. Where he picked up the cross is the last station on the way to the cross for you to visit if you are ever in Jerusalem.

Barabbas was a robber, a murderer and rebel. He was the leader of a band of legionaries that sought to save the Jews from Roman rule. In character, Barabbas represents the devil!

He is mentioned in Matt. 27:17-26; Mark 5:15; Luke 23:18-23; but the Book of John does not mention him.

Goliath is the best-known giant in the bible. He is described as a champion warrior out of the camp of the Philistines, who was over nine feet tall. A literal interpretation of the verses in the book of Samuel suggest that his brother and three sons were giants also. The third son's name does not appear in the bible --so I have named him Hexadactylies; as it was said that he had six fingers on each hand and six toes on each foot (2nd Samuel 21:20-21).

The Philistines mustered their army to do battle against the army of Israel. There was only a valley separating them when Goliath came out to fight (read for yourselves what he was wearing for battle in 1st Samuel 17:4-7).

He shouted to the Israelites, "There is no need for all of you to die. I am the Philistine champion, but you are only the servants of Saul. CHOOSE ONE MAN TO COME FIGHT ME! If he kills me, we will be your slaves. But if I kill him, you will be our slaves." To know who won this battle and by what means, you have to read it for yourselves!

As I finish with the writing of this book, I leave you with a challenge. There are five men, whose name appear only once in the Bible and all are mentioned together in one single verse. The men were: Sopater, a kinsman of Paul. Secundus a Thessalonian, Gaius, the Greek spelling for the Roman name Caius, Tychicus, who was alluded to have been with Paul in Rome, and Trophimus, who caused Paul to be imprisoned.

Where is this one verse located in the bible?

Eutychus was a young man of Troas tended to by Saint Paul. He fell asleep due to the long nature of the discourse Paul was giving and fell from a window out of the three-story building and died. Let this be a lesson to you who often close your eyes during a church service! Paul will not be there to revive you!

Made in the USA
Monee, IL
21 May 2023

34112798R10079